THE RUINS OF NOSTALGIA

Donna Stonecipher

the RUINS *of* NOSTALGIA

Wesleyan University Press | Middletown, Connecticut

Wesleyan University Press

Middletown CT 06459

www.wesleyan.edu/wespress

2023 © Donna Stonecipher

All rights reserved

Manufactured in the United States of America

Designed by Mindy Basinger Hill

Typeset in Adobe Caslon Pro

Library of Congress Cataloging-in-Publication Data
available upon request

Hardcover ISBN: 978-0-8195-0083-0

Paperback ISBN: 978-0-8195-0084-7

Ebook ISBN: 978-0-8195-0085-4

5   4   3   2   1

Our imagination . . . leads us unexpectedly into cities or theatres, plains or meadows. We may further observe, when the fancy thus reflects on the scenes that have past in it formerly, those, which were at first pleasant to behold, appear more so upon reflection, and that the memory heightens the delightfulness of the original.

JOSEPH ADDISON | from "The Pleasures of the Imagination," no. 417

Nostalgia is at the very core of the modern condition

SVETLANA BOYM

Only other men's nostalgias offend

RAYMOND WILLIAMS

THE RUINS OF NOSTALGIA

Courtyard opened out into courtyard opened out into courtyard, and in the final courtyard, an art gallery was closing. It had opened shortly after the fall of the Wall, incandescent with idealism. Tonight was the opening of its closing exhibition.   *   What is art for? To critique society, to manufacture beauty, to make the artist lose all sense of time like a malfunctioning hourglass through which the sand just keeps pouring and pouring?   *   *When I get a little money I buy books, if I have any left over I buy food and clothing.* —Erasmus. This was printed on a bookmark tucked into each book she'd bought at the bookstore she used to frequent in her youth, which was closing. At this bookstore, courtyard after courtyard had opened in her mind. The bookstore was wood-paneled, with a spiral staircase winding up to fiction, and a spiral staircase winding down to nonfiction. At this bookstore, she had felt incandescent with idealism. *   "One door closes, another opens": a commonplace. The art gallery was closing; the bookstore was closing; but when their doors closed, the commonplace said, other doors would open. Other commonplaces. "The market takes care of itself."   *   It was only at night, sometimes, that she realized that the door in the saying wasn't really a door, it was only sgraffito, and the series of courtyards wasn't really a series of courtyards, it was only a recurring dream of never arriving, walking permanently through archway after archway into the ruins of nostalgia.

We had been to the secret service museum, to the shredded-documents-being-pieced-back-together museum, to the museum of the wealthy family's Biedermeier house from 1830, to the museum of the worker family's apartment from 1905, to the museum of the country that no longer exists, to the museum of the history of the post office, to the museum of the history of clocks. We had seen the bracelets made of the beloved's hair, the Kaiserpanorama, the pneumatic tubes, the hourglasses, the shreds, the microphones hidden in the toupees, the ticking, the gilded mirrors reflecting our faces, the two rooms eight people lived in, the eight rooms two people lived in, the shreds, the trays of frangible butterflies carrying freight, the silvery clepsydras, the ticking, the simulacra, the shreds, the vitrines, the velvet ropes, the idealized portraits of the powerful, the blurry photographs of the powerless, the shreds, the erasures, the eras, the sureties, the ticking, the pink façades, the upward mobility, the shreds, the plunging fortunes, the downward spirals, the ticking, the ticking, the shreds, the shreds. We had been to the museum of the ruins of nostalgia.

Four deer stood poised down in a valley as the train passed by, like four artworks in a museum, framed in the rectangular windows of the train, a tableau vivant that hardly changes no matter how many times the train passes, heading north or heading south, for the poised deer are the same poised deer that stood there a century ago, the streams ferrying their cargo of dead twigs are the same streams as two centuries ago, the trees felled and planted and tended and felled and planted and tended, and felled, the foresters still sculptural and storied, the kids in the woods flirting with addiction to crystal, crystals forming on the windows of the train carrying the cargo of passengers whose bloodstreams ferry the cargo of antidepressants, antihistamines, anticoagulants, anti-inflammatories, passengers who keep glancing out at the museum of nature, reminding themselves *I've been meaning to visit that exhibit*, that exhibit where the deer are waiting for us and not waiting, where the trees are waiting for us and not waiting, where the wildflowers still under the earth are waiting and not waiting for spring to force them out into morbidly orderly inflorescence, where the origin is and is not waiting for its impurity, and a crystal palace whose roof fell in on itself from its own weight years ago still houses the ruins of nostalgia.

We didn't miss mercers or chandlers, and anyway the world was still full of silk cloth and candles. We didn't miss coopers or smiths. We didn't miss elevator boys or indexers, haberdashers or confectioners or lady's maids or almoners. We didn't miss typists. We didn't miss scriveners. So would we really miss doctors and lawyers and accountants when the day came, and the radio tonight said it was coming, when their expertise was surpassed by software?   *   We didn't miss the assembly line. We didn't miss data entry. Did we miss switchboard operators? No, because we had too many photos of them. We did miss lamplighters, a little, because we missed the ornate iron gas lamps they had lit in the evenings, as we missed carrying flickering candles up to our rooms in our nightgowns, banking the fires in our hearths, out our windows the liquid vantablack of night, nightly flooding and drowning lux perpetua. We had missed it—we had missed the lamplighters and the candles and the banking and the snuffing. We had missed the labor of light.   *   Would we miss truck drivers? Would we miss flesh-and-blood babysitters, teenage girls that the fathers would drive home in their Volvos in states of sexual tension they would evanesce later, back home with their wives?   *   Software was so . . . so very soft. We would miss software. We wouldn't miss hardware, though. We would secure for software the softest of soft spots among the ruins of nostalgia.

She drove downtown and got disoriented. There was a forest of towering new towers refracting the familiar landscape, erasing the turns and curves she'd long followed unconsciously in her car, to get downtown, where now there was a forest of towers, where once had been only forest. She parked, and got disoriented. The low, ornamented, turn-of-the-century buildings were being wrecking-balled to oblivion to make way for towering new glass towers, wedged between one-way streets like the one she'd driven up the wrong way as a timid teenager in a blue Hornet picking up her sister from her summer job (selling ice cream in the old outdoor market) (saved from the wrecking ball by citizens' initiative, 1971). * She tried to find the ice cream shop, but got disoriented. * She drove to a neighboring neighborhood and got disoriented—there was the blue bascule bridge, but what was it bridging? Two halves that did not make a whole. She crossed back to the canal where the poplars of her childhood had all been felled, felled, the canal now canal-front—canal-front property—for new residents paying to muse upon the mutability of moving water. * She drove to the wooden house she'd been born in on the ridge, with little windows not showcasing the picturesque mountain view (little windows because nobody cared back then about views) (had once elucidated her father) (who'd grown up in the house with no view on the ridge) and got disoriented, for now each house on the ridge had had its back or front wrecking-balled to make way for picture windows giving the new residents a permanent picture of the picturesque mountains—and—were they visible?—of the mounting ruins of her nostalgia.

Nostalgia feels personal as a pearl feels personal in its shell, never knowing that beyond it are thousands of other mollusks depositing nacreous layers over parasites in thousands of other shells. * Many people remember the downtown of a neighborhood from their youth, with its dowdy department store and its five-and-dime, but one person is nostalgic for the clove cigarettes you could buy one at a time from a glass jar, another is nostalgic for the little blue Bakelite birds that cost a quarter, a third is nostalgic for the doughnut shop that became a Thai restaurant (and a fourth is nostalgic for the Thai restaurant, which became a vegan doughnut shop). * True, looking backward can either cause you to miss what's ahead or envelop you in a warmth so contingent you understand how a coat can be made of translucent ashes. Every pearl is on a continuum with a parasite. * A fifth person was nostalgic for the dowdy downtown just because he knew the new people drinking and shopping in the new downtown were not, could not be nostalgic for it, because they had no idea it had ever existed. Ah, but they could. They could be nostalgic for a downtown they had no idea had ever existed. Because nostalgia is specific yet indiscriminate, benign yet opportunistic, personal yet collective, and if the twentieth century taught us anything, it's that anyone feels welcome to wander through the ruins of anyone else's nostalgia.

Even if unconsciously, the city's inhabitants had been glad of the holes. Empty slots between buildings, empty lots on corners, where here a handmade bar, there an impromptu park had been wedged between brick walls, or the green grass had just been left to expand unchecked. Even if unconsciously, the inhabitants had been glad of the empty lots, which had seemed permanent, rendered the city permeable; the ease of them, the way the holes allowed the whole to breathe, the city's inhabitants to breathe more easily, for if there was surplus space, then surely there was surplus time, lots and slots of unoccupied and unmaximized time to fill the holes and empty them again. Or so it had seemed.   *   Of course it was a little odd to be glad of the bombs that had blown the buildings to bits, to be grateful for the failed bankrupt state that had enabled the holes to remain holes, so lying on the grass of an accidental playground, one just listened to the ping-pong ball batted back and forth across the concrete table. And thought idly of one's own surpluses and deficits.   *   And then, one day, one of the city's holes that had seemed permanent was filled. Not long after that, overnight—a few more. And then still more. More people, it seemed, wanted to become inhabitants of the city marked by surplus space and time. More people than there was surplus space for. The people who had moved a long time ago to the city marked by surplus space and time looked at the people who were now moving to the city marked by surplus space and time, who would soon be looking at people moving to a city no longer marked by surplus space and time.   *   And suddenly any remaining empty lots turned into sites of projection and desire. Because as soon as a hole was filled, it was gone, seemingly never to return. And soon the city would no longer seem permeable. And this would seem permanent. *   Content, it turned out, was not synonymous with form; some forms of content blew some forms of form to bits. Empty form was just formal. A surplus of people wanted surplus space and time, which swiftly used up the surplus space, which meant the surplus time was gone, too; never to return. And so it goes in the ruins of nostalgia.

First someone invented a word designating nostalgia for life in East Germany: *Ostalgie*. Then someone else made a movie called *Ostalgie*. Then other people opened an *Ostalgie*-themed hotel where guests could stay in rooms with faded pink patterned wallpaper and orange phones with a special button for *Volkspolizei*. Of the people, for the people, by the people. "A country does not have friends, it has interests" (Charles De Gaulle). And sometimes maybe even people do not have friends, they have interests. And maybe a population does not even have people, it has interests. The *Volkspolizei* seemed the dream of a people who would discipline themselves and never need to peer into the mirror and say: fuck the police. But long after the *Volkspolizei*'s demise, when six hundred policepeople enforced the eviction of eleven anarchists from a squatted building on Brunnenstrasse whose billionaire needed it back, what button was there to push? Curtains hung in the windows; rent was paid; the Umsonst Laden on the ground floor saw influx and outflux of stuff without influx and outflux of cash; "Wir bleiben alle" read the façade. * No one knows where the anarchists are now, the Umsonst Laden melted away like smudged snow in spring, and the building stood empty for years, only a few pigeons nesting in the derelict splendors of the ruins of nostalgia.

We watched a video on the internet of the arena we'd seen our first concert in being bulldozed. We had seen no video of the club where we'd first smoked clove cigarettes and kissed a boy wearing makeup bulldozed. One day it was just no longer there. We had seen no video or photos of our high school being bulldozed. When we heard that our elementary school was scheduled for the wrecking ball we walked down and took photos of the mural of a deer in a snowy landscape we'd won a contest to get to paint on the school wall. Shortly after, the deer was bulldozed. We had seen no photos of the café where we had first drunk a mocha bulldozed. One day it was just no longer there. We had been astonished to find a real café, with real intellectuals in it playing chess, real Persian cats draped on sills, real mochas and cappuccinos and disheveled newspapers on poles and foxed wallpaper in our own provincial city. By the time the café was bulldozed ten years later, we weren't astonished. We had not seen any photos or videos of it bulldozed; one day, it was just no longer there. In that bulldozed café and other bulldozed cafés around the city we'd always ordered mochas, which bridged our childish love of sweets with our lust for adult narcotics. We had not seen many photos or videos of the sites across which our youth had played out bulldozed, but one by one they must all have been, for one day they were just no longer there.   *   Sometimes we felt sheepish for listing the sites of our youth that had been bulldozed to make room for the bulging of prosperity. But the question of who was really prospering did not stand long before it was bulldozed. Any attempt to turn around and glance one last time at the past resulted in that past being instantly bulldozed, bulldozed, bulldozed. For the bulls never doze in the ruins of nostalgia.

A woman began to fall prey to bouts of nostalgia for the world of her youth, which was the world her mother had just been entering when she began to fall prey to bouts of nostalgia for the world of her youth, which was the world *her* mother had just been entering when she began to fall prey to bouts of nostalgia for the world of her youth, which was the world *her* mother had just been entering when she began to fall prey to bouts of nostalgia for the world of her youth, which was the world *her* mother had just been entering when she began to fall prey to bouts of nostalgia for the world of her youth, which was the world . . .

We were able to be nostalgic both for certain cultural phenomena that had vanished, and for the time before the cultural phenomena had appeared, as if every world we lived in hid another world behind it, like stage scenery of a city hiding stage scenery of tiered meadows hiding stage scenery of ancient Illyria. For example it wasn't answering machines, or the lack of answering machines, or the sight of tiny answering-machine tape cassettes that triggered our nostalgia, but the realization that our lives had transcended the brief life of the answering machine, had preceded and succeeded it, encompassed it, swallowed it whole, which meant we had to understand ourselves not as contained entities, but as planes intersecting with other planes, planes of time, technology, culture, desire. One plane had waited by the phone for our best friend's phone call before answering machines, and then one plane had recorded outgoing messages on the answering machine over and over, trying and trying to sound blithe. How many tiny tape cassettes still stored pieces of our voices like pale-blue fragments of Plexiglas shattered into attics and basements across any number of states? We still owned a tape cassette with the voice of our first beloved on it, or a version of it, and remembered the version of the girl who kept rewinding his messages over and over, under an analogue wedge of black sky and endlessly delayed stars. She was listening and listening for answers the answering machine could not provide. When we felt our material planes sliding to intersect with immaterial planes, or vice versa, we bowed our heads and submitted to the pile-up of the ruins of nostalgia.

Some inhabitants of a city were milling around a room one sunny day looking at an exhibit of historical maps of earlier iterations of their city, all carrying fragile nostalgias in their minds, which they all thought of as the only possible nostalgia, but in fact they were inhabiting a city radiating with multiple and multilexical and multistratigraphic nostalgias. * The structure was concentric. Newer inhabitants, whose nostalgia was on the inner rings, tended to talk about it more. One brand-new inhabitant at a dinner party, possibly on coke, was so nostalgic that he wasn't even nostalgic for the past, but for the present, a kind of pre-order nostalgia, because he knew *it couldn't last, it couldn't last,* he kept repeating, shaking his head, his wide eyes staring glazed at the table. Couldn't last? It's already over! thought the rest of the guests, who were longer-term inhabitants. But they sipped their wine in silence, for their nostalgias—also, of course, the only possible nostalgias—were on wider rings. * The city's maps were usually kept in the dark, in an archive, in flat files, their ornamental lettering and pale pink and yellow shaded quadrants and their schematized trees and their utopian onanisms and their erasures and their projections, silenced in flat files like the most tenderly ideological utterances. Each map, made of star matter, was the only possible map. * The city streets pulsed with this secret retrogressive melancholy preoccupation, with the rings of its inhabitants' multiple nostalgias, widening and widening. But what was at the center of the concentric rings? Was it the same thing that was at the center of trees' rings? Or at the center of rings widening out from an unknown catalyst on a lake? * Was the center of nostalgia an absence, or was the nostalgia for absence a center, around which to build a liquid orientation, a concentrically spreading stain of emotional acquiescence? * "The sunlight came into the room with the peacefulness one remembers from rooms in one's early childhood—a sunlight encountered later only in one's dreams" (James Baldwin). * But wasn't it rather a kind of cold starlight bathing the ruins of the only possible nostalgia?

Where once there had been a low-end stationery store minded by an elderly beauty queen, there was now a store for high-end espresso machines minded by nobody. Where once there had been an illegal beer garden in a weedy lot, there was now a complex of luxury lofts with Parisian-style ivory façades. Where once there had been a bookstore and a bike shop and a bakery, there was now a wax museum for tourists. Where once there had been an empty lot there was now a building. Where once there had been an empty lot there was now a building. Where once there had been an empty lot there was now a building. Where once there had been an empty lot there was now a building. Where once there had been farms there were now subdivisions. Where once there had been subdivisions there were now sub-subdivisions. We lived in a sub-subdivision of a subdivision. We ourselves had become subdivided—where once we had merely been of two minds. * Where once there had been a river there was now a road. A vocal local group had started a movement to break up the road and "daylight" the river, which still flowed, in the dark, underneath the road. * Could we daylight the farms, the empty lots, the stationery store, the elderly beauty queen, the city we moved to? Was it still flowing somewhere, under the luxury lofts, deliquescing in the dark, inhabited by our luxury selves, not yet subdivided, because not yet whole? * Could we daylight the ruins of nostalgia?

We did not know anyone who had grown up in our neighborhood who could now afford to live in our neighborhood. None of us could afford to rent a house in our neighborhood, much less buy a house or even an apartment in a converted garage in our neighborhood. Over the years, the houses in our neighborhood had kept changing hands. They gained second stories, third stories, picture windows and skylights, hot tubs and balconies, gained terraces and gardens, lost yards, lost rhododendrons, gained sedge and lavender, lost juniper bushes, gained butterfly bushes and chard. We watched as houses in our neighborhood were knocked down and replaced by bigger houses, houses so big there was no room for a garden or a yard, big houses squeezed uneasily into their too-small lots, story stacked on story topped with a flat roof in a neighborhood of small houses with pitched roofs. Pitched roofs to shrug off the rain that had been hushing down since before our neighborhood was built, and that would be hushing down long after our neighborhood had all been knocked down. * And yet—in truth—we were not certain we knew exactly what "our neighborhood" meant. Did "our neighborhood" mean our neighbors, or the houses our neighbors had lived in, or the street grid, or some combination of the above? As our neighborhood gained infill, lost empty lots, lost gas guzzlers, gained hatchbacks, gained SUVs, gained cafés, lost taverns, lost movie theaters, lost children playing in the intersections, we had atomized to ever more distant suburbs, suburbs with names mangled from Native American names, or mimicking European names, or invented to evoke elevated and inviting names. * Nevertheless, there persisted a delicate web of connection between us and the people who had also grown up in our neighborhood. This web was not a real web, and yet it was a real web. Undoubtedly there was also such a web connecting the people who'd grown up in the suburban neighborhoods we now lived in, which *they* could no longer afford. (And who were now atomized to ever more distant suburbs.) * A few of our parents still lived in the small houses with pitched roofs we had grown up in in our neighborhood. When we visited these houses, and helped our mothers beat back the burgeoning butterfly bushes, we felt buried alive in the ruins of nostalgia. They were not real ruins, and yet they were real ruins.

If nostalgia is primarily aesthetic, i.e., if a beautiful moment we experienced but were not able to apprehend could be apprehended post-hoc, then the impossibility of living in the present could be slathered over with a layer of gold-suffused salve, SALVE, as the blue-and-white tiles spelled out before the door to the barber shop in the city of our youth, for which we feel nostalgic. Repeat. The barber is dead; long live the barber. The city of our youth no longer exists; it exists in our minds. The barber's pinup calendars are smoldering their way down the landfill. Johannes Hofer believed that nostalgia could be cured with opium, leeches, or a trip to the Alps, but we know that the only cure for nostalgia is nostalgia. There is an illness informing the illness, and that illness must be mined to extract the exquisitely atavistic elixir. We kept walking through the beautiful city in our minds saying, *Stay, thou art so fair*, but the city did not comply. We walked and walked through the city in our minds infecting and healing ourselves at the same time, infecting and healing, infecting and healing, until it was impossible to tell the difference, until we were totally infected, and totally healed. But as soon as we left the city in our minds to come back to this city, we knew that the healing was temporary, and the infection forever.   *   If nostalgia is primarily aesthetic, then it is also unstable, and if we get attached to beautiful images today, we might spurn them tomorrow. We might love the beautiful images because we can't apprehend them, "the beautiful" always relocating itself, unrecognizable as the city outside, which is why we keep trying to rebuild the city in our minds. And it's why we slather salve over SALVE, suffuse it, why we gold-leaf gold leaf. It's why we ruin the ruins of nostalgia.

"Luxus für alle!" read the signs held by many hands at the demonstration against the luxury-loft developers—luxury for all, light for all, like the light blue crazed light of the sky in the Caspar David Friedrich painting in the museum across the bridge, fragile, cracking, one of the museums that used to stay open for free Thursday nights for the city's penniless aesthetes, till tour buses started landing like fleets of sleek spaceships disgorging bored EU teenagers who giggled through the ornate restored rooms, and it occurred to somebody that two EU teenagers in the hand are worth more than a local Romantic in the bush. Caspar David Friedrich für alle! Prussian Romanticism für alle! Backs of pensive figures with tilted heads looking out at the moon für alle! Snowy Christian symbolism für alle, shipwrecks, ruins, dark forests, lonely monks für alle, crazed fragile blue heaven crazed heaven für alle. * If we thought some aspects of the previous system were better than those of the current system, were we just "nostalgic" for the previous system? If we wished the empty lots would stay empty lots and not become luxury lofts, were we just "nostalgic" for empty lots? We wondered how many sources had been banking on narratives of progress as an enervating force, and how inscribed our minds were with these narratives; we wondered if nostalgia was not, in fact, a symptom of progress, but if both progress and nostalgia were symptoms of centuries of systems tilting their heads at stylized shipwrecks under the moon. * The people at the demonstration were certain that we were all born ineluctably into Luxus— cracked fragile blue heavenly state in which the ruins of nostalgia might even be the apogee of progress.

As a child we dialed "SU2-8598" to call home, SU two, eight five nine eight, and the letters—SU—stood for Sunset: Sunset two, eight five nine eight, our phone number had a sunset in it, a sunset forever in the act of performing its orange gradations, built right into the phone number, which was not a phone number at all—but a scene, a scene with a number articulated into it, a scene with a sun that glowed once like an ember each time we articulated our phone number. There were also phone numbers that began LA (Lakeview) and AT (Atwater) and EM (Emerson), and so each phone number began with letters standing for a word that conjured an image offering the dialer a scene setting in which to imagine: the telephone, located, the person answering the telephone, located, sitting perhaps at a little wooden table specially designed for telephoning, performing her orange gradations into the phone, in the background a sunset, in the background a lake view, in the background a neighborhood named for a Transcendental philosopher. We didn't know why, over time, the usage changed, and the sunset was dropped from the number, and the scene went dark, the childhood phone number went dark, the sunset dropping down and down to the end of the sky, the childhood phone number went dark, the sun setting and setting and the lake view obscured by a set of numbers with no letters, the sun setting into the setting that was dismantling, nothing transcending nothing, the sun setting fast behind the woman sitting at a dismantling telephone table in the onset of the dark. Now she is only locatable in the ruins of nostalgia.

Trying to escape our own ruins, we took a train and then a ferry to someone else's, Friedrich Wilhelm der Zweite's, on the Peacock Island—still feathery with peacocks. *   A crumbling white castle occupied one end of the island, and a dairy built to look like the ruins of a Gothic cloister anchored the other.   *   At this dairy Wilhelm's fifteen-year-old wife, Wilhelmine, played milkmaid, lost in the aristocratic vogue for the simple country life. And this dairy, we found, was just as ruined as the day it was built in 1794, in the aristocratic vogue for ruins. We found the peacocks' blue beauty ruinous, as we were meant to. We found the ruin of the dairy still new centuries later, preserved in the same state of ruin as centuries ago. Like milk in centuries of ice. Or was it the tiniest bit more ruined?   *   Do fake ruins age more slowly than real ruins? If real ruins intrigue us by foretelling our own ruin, I said, why do fake ruins, which tell us we can live forever, interest us so little? The fake ruin, you said, was invented just before the advent of modern bureaucracy. Which was around the same time the *vanitas* was dying out, the skull or hourglass placed among scenes of lavishly unraveling lemons, goblets, fresh-killed rabbits.   *   O what did it mean? That if we did not attend to our own ruin we would end up milked like the fake dairy, trapped in the nostalgia for ruins amid the ageless ruins of nostalgia?

They left one monumental worker statue on a wide sidewalk where there was room, but melted down most of the others. The worker in boots and overalls hailed a city that slowly forgot him, that secretly wanted him to be forgotten, as new glass buildings rose all around, the linden trees blossomed and obscured his hailing hand, and traffic whisked people every which way away from him.   *   Traffic has no teleological conclusion; the overgrown cemetery kitty-corner had stopped accepting new tenants; and a neglected trove of broken gravestones in the far corner all read WIR VERGESSEN DICH NIE (except for one broken into two: WIR VERGESSEN DICH / NIE).   *   And yet somebody did forget—those who would never forget, ever forgot, or were ever forgotten in their turn. A promise is a trove of little unbroken permissions to forget, and don't all promisers know it.   *   The worker was left "for the tourists," but as the years stopped tending the distance between the worker and the emotional work he was meant to do, fewer and fewer tourists knew what work to do with him, what he signified, why he was so outsize and ostentatiously dignified. And so we weren't surprised one day when we walked by and found him missing.   *   May this poem ever forget him forever.   *   Was he melted down? Like so many other enigmas of the ruins of nostalgia?

For a long time we'd listened to the stories of those who had lived in countries that no longer existed, and the stories had been exciting—stories of privation, of deprivation, of limits, of lack. But after a time we had heard the same stories so many times that even the tellers grew weary of the telling. "Nobody had telephones—we just left messages on notepads attached to people's doors" (mm-hm). "I wasn't allowed to go to university, because I did x (harmless thing)" (mm-hm). "Everyone was having affairs, because the private life was the only realm in which you felt free" (mm-hm). When we realized we had heard the same stories so many times that there remained only a residual excitement to the telling, we grew melancholy, mostly for the storytellers and their unexciting stories, but also for ourselves—for at one time the stories had excited us into the aesthetic of the empathetic: we had felt the shocks of forms of injustice new to us, and had enjoyed bristling with outrage that need not become action. These stories had briefly become our stories—it was our phonelessness, deprivations, limits, lacks. And the stories had revealed that our current splendid plenitude lacked the poetics of lack. And lack, it turned out, revealed its own splendid plenitude . . . * It was only once it was no longer possible that we realized how good it had felt to nestle into the ruins of someone else's nostalgia.

It was before the city built traffic circles at every intersection to prevent accidents, like the one she'd heard one Sunday afternoon that sounded like someone shoving her parents' stereo to the floor, but she'd run downstairs to find the stereo intact, her brother in front of it as usual, practicing "Stairway to Heaven" on the guitar, headphones on. Out in the intersection was the woman, driving alone, who'd caused the accident, in her thirties, sitting on the curb, in shock. And then the police came. It was after all that.   * One day after that the city came and built the traffic circles, one per intersection, which spelled the end of traffic accidents, but also spelled the end of the neighborhood kids' evening games of kickball in the intersection, the sewer lids at each corner serving as bases, the countless balls lost in the brambly thicket in the yard of the old woman living alone, where sometimes a curtain was yanked aside and the kids all screamed and tore down the block. And then the voices of mothers and fathers calling from porches up and down the street: Terry – Shelly – Tommy – Carol – Darlene –. And after meat loaf and cake from boxes they would reconvene to play hide-and-seek around the intersection or sit on the rockery and talk shit about the kids who claimed to have had sex or whose parents were divorcing. It was all before the intersection was no longer an intersection, but an obstacle. It was before young kids said "talk shit." It was after the company town started hemorrhaging residents when the company's profits plunged. It was after the kids would call "Car!" when a rare evening gas guzzler was seen about to drive through their kickball game. It was before the gas guzzler was understood as a gas guzzler. It was after tail fins, it was before hatchbacks. It was before a neighbor girl was hit by a car down the street and covered with a sheet.   * It was before the intersection was recognized as an intersection of kids from divergent backgrounds and family tragedies working out the rules of mostly harmonious kickball games. It was before anyone might have thought much about the sociology of intersections. It was after the troubling number of traffic accidents at intersections. It was before the troubling absence of children playing at intersections. It was before the last kickball got lost in the thicket of the ruins of nostalgia.

She felt nostalgic for the time when ballet dancers, ice skaters, and gymnasts from behind the Iron Curtain had defected from East to West. As a child she'd sat at home Saturday mornings coveting Nadia Comaneci's hair bows on American TV, and watched as ballet dancers, ice skaters, and gymnasts twirled out from a grim gray ground of poverty and tight control, or so she was told on TV, with their exquisite bodies, their exquisitely precise bodies, exquisitely precisely disciplined bodies (more disciplined than in the West, because who needs discipline when you are "free"?) into her imprecise and undisciplined Saturday mornings watching TV. * The word "defected" had made her think of "infected," or of an abbreviation of "disinfected," the disciplined ballet dancers, ice skaters, and gymnasts had disinfected from the East to the undisciplined West, so scrupulously disaffected, and got added to a collection of Iron Curtain dolls that twirled and twirled the gray from their pink toe shoes, their hand-sewn costumes, their accents, their blackening lungs, or so she was told, on TV. * As they defected, she cathected. She imagined tutus torn on barbed wire, furious officials fuming in fusty offices, getaway Corvettes, exhilaration mingled with tears. Somehow she understood that she would never have to be that disciplined—or that brave—but she did not understand why. * Discipline, yes, but also drugs, it turned out later, discipline and drugs, State Plan 14.25, e.g., but then everyone, East and West, North and South, was on drugs, despite the "war on drugs," though not everyone was disciplined, because how much discipline do you need when you are already free. * Now the Iron Curtain was dismantled, there was no need to defect anymore, twirling from East to West, and she wondered if the word "defect" was now, essentially, defunct—like her old TV set was defunct, like the war on drugs was defunct, like the Cold War was defunct, like "East" and "West" and Corvettes were defunct, like her childhood and everything in it was defunct. But then a friend pointed out a building in an East European capital as one of many owned by Katarina Witt, "the Most Beautiful Face of Socialism," and she saw like an X-ray straight through the flickering blue windows to the ruins of her exquisitely undisciplined nostalgia.

We found ourselves, to our astonishment, living on and on past the past. We wondered if it was, in the cosmic sense, accidental that "nostalgia" begins with "no." Johannes Hofer, Swiss medical student, may not have had "no" in mind when coining the word "nostalgia," but treasuries used to believe that coining new currency would beat back down engulfing debt. Nostalgia coins sentiment into durable objects that can be traded in markets of feeling jarred like honey. The exchequer clouds coin raindrops, which are absorbed by dirt, which coins the currencies of grain. Who felt nostalgic before there was nostalgia? From his coign of vantage Cortez, it is said, was overwhelmed by nostalgia for the beauty of Aztec cities just before he destroyed them. The profiles on gold coins, we could say, coined the obliquity of greed. It's no wonder the Spaniards never found Eldorado, since it is always located behind us.   *   Does one destroy the past just by living past it? If that is true, then nostalgia may be the only currency we have with which to repay the debts we owe to what we have left behind. — To those whom we have left behind.   *   Even as nostalgia coins a "no" each time we fall, with a "yes," into the defaulting vaults of the ruins of nostalgia.

The oldest house in the neighborhood is for sale. The oldest house in the neighborhood, owned by the state garden club, has been put up for sale. Queen-Anne-style, with leaded-glass windows, and a turret, the house has been put up for sale by the state garden club, to whom it was bequeathed, in 1977, by the ladies' improvement club. The bequeathal included a clause that included the clause that the Queen-Anne-style house, and its pear orchards, be preserved by the state garden club "forever." Nevertheless, the state garden club has put up the oldest house in the neighborhood for sale. The house is, was, is, no longer listed on the National Register of Historic Places. The garden club went to court to ask for a lifting of the listing on the National Register of Historic Places. Because the upkeep of the oldest house in the neighborhood, with its leaded-glass windows, and its pear orchards, and its historic-ness, is onerous. For forty years the garden club tended its pear orchards, and its garden, and intended to preserve its pears and its leaded-glass windows and its turret "forever." Forever? Forever. Forever? Forever. Pears are preserved into preserves. A historic place is preserved into a Historic Place. A tower slurs into a turret. The oldest house in the neighborhood, with its leaded-glass windows and its garden, sits on a lot that could contain an apartment building with "30 to 40 units" in a city with an acute affordable-housing shortage. But the house was bequeathed "forever." But the house, the house, with its leaded-glass windows and its garden, its 135 years of existence. Its 135 years of pears. Its preservation. But the "30 to 40 units." The court allowed the listing to be lifted because the ladies' improvement club was dissolved in 1983, and no ladies were left to protest it. But a lady from the state garden club board did resign in protest, an 88-year-old lady named Lona. But Lona. But the 30 to 40 units. But the pear orchards. But the new families. But the leaded glass. But the ladies, improving and improving. But the Queen-Anne-style house. But the obsolescence of queens. But the history, the Historic Place. But the city's acute affordable-housing shortage—the homeless people lining the freeways. But the stories the house could tell, if it could tell. But Lona. But the neighborhood groups now scrambling to buy the house. What are they trying to preserve? The house, the past, the old neighborhood, the historic place, history? And Lona? But Lona. But the house— the large, old, antiquated, elegant, beloved, hated, fragile-as-an-eggshell house, which escaped fire, earthquakes, the meticulous dismantlings of time, of everything except "prosperity." Built 135 years ago for shelter, will the shelter now be sheltered? But the 30 to 40 units. But Lona. But Lona. But the pear orchard, the garden, the turret, the leaded glass, the house, the house.

In the fall we were nostalgic for the summer. In the winter we were nostalgic for the fall. In the summer we were nostalgic for the spring. But in the spring we were not nostalgic for the winter, not even for its quiet, or its hot cocoas, or its video fires, though we did ask our father from time to time to tell us about how, when he was a child, the man-made lake in the middle of our city froze over every winter, and how one December day he broke through the ice and was only saved from drowning by a neighbor boy whose name he can no longer remember. We were nostalgic for the frozen lake we had never seen, that is, for the lake we had never seen frozen, the man-made lake we had swum in during the summers after the lake froze. It was hard to imagine the summer lake frozen. It was hard to imagine the winter lake summery. It was hard to imagine the lake being made, and not just spontaneously welling up its murky green effluence. We were nostalgic for winters that had descended before we were sentient, as if those winters existed in snow globes we could stow on our nightstands and dream of falling and falling through the ice we are always rescued from by neighbors who become strangers over time. The lake is always melting in the ruins of nostalgia.

She liked to walk past a building she used to live in when she was young, when there were 100,000 empty apartments in the city, it was said, before foreign money jetted in and bought up most of them. She had seen it at an airport somewhere once: a sign over a desk: FOREIGN MONEY. * Can lurking around scenes of youthful happiness warm one with a reconstructed glow, like the eight-hour YouTube video of a fire in a fireplace she and her boyfriend fired up each weekend that winter, that crackled, spat, and snapped in a reassuringly long loop—but never quite long enough, for around hour five one of them would get nervous and go click the video back to the beginning . . . * Many types of simulacra can warm one, it is said. * A fire is kept in the fireplace. A market is kept in its marketplace. * She walked past the cream-colored building with one balcony atop an oriel and thought of her young self living a life that was hers and somebody else's, like watching herself in a YouTube video watching a YouTube video of a fire in a fireplace, or looking at herself on a stereoscope card, herself and herself, at a slightly shifted angle, "living" her "life" like "dying" a "slow" "death," firing up a fire, monetizing money, homing in on a home—long gone, monetized, o exchequer, FOREIGN MONEY. * There was the cemetery with the long allées of plane trees she'd used as an office, the memorial screwed to the wall across the street, the unrenovated courtyards people were always vanishing into, perhaps leading to some of the 100,000 empty apartments (it was said), all renovated now, all occupied, all vanished. The A Bar at one end of the street, and the Z Bar at the other. * But the A Bar was no longer called the A Bar. And the Z Bar wasn't exactly at its zenith. * It wasn't "a" Z Bar, it was "the" Z Bar. It was "the" allées, "the" memorial, it wasn't "an" A Bar. Was nostalgia "the," and not-nostalgia "a"? Was being young knowing there were 100,000 empty apartments in your city? It was said? * To whom was FOREIGN MONEY foreign? * To whom was FOREIGN MONEY domestic? * The marketplace wants to be warmed by the fireplace. The building she used to live in was a commonplace. Her pockets were a commonplace. She walked up and down the street with her pockets full of FOREIGN MONEY, rubbing herself all over the ruins of her nostalgia.

It's not hard to see why nostalgia rose with modern bureaucracy, with the forward arrow charting irreversible time rather than arcing lazily into circles, for without records there would be no luscious glance backward into the translucent gold bars of things we experienced in an arrangement of variables that looked like history, but was actually hagiography.   *   As the names and dates were set down, gold-leaf haloes were superadded to possessions we didn't actually possess, the past slowly reified into objects we could not bear to leave behind. Objects stamped and stamped with gold leaf. Isn't it easier to possess a past that will never return, than a past that will?   *   The files were filed into systems that filtered the silica out of the quartz with the aid of sand, the most bureaucratic of materials, slipping and slipping through the wasp waists of the sixteenth century's most accurate chronometers. What have you done with the time, we ask the sand. Falling over and over through the hourglass reversed unto perpetuity. What have you done with the past, we ask the gold leaf, and as we ask it the ruins of nostalgia get stamped with a halo.

It started with a small voice sounding in the wilderness about spotted owls, no louder than a low hoot from the owl itself, recorded in the forest by a devout birder. There was an ever-smaller number of owls, the voice said, flitting through the trees, their heads revolving like feathered sirens signaling the emergency that their habitat was shrinking to extinction. Then the voice grew louder, and then other voices answered, louder still. The voices asked: is an owl more important than a person? The forests had been clear-cut, one by one. We saw the mountains' shaved patches, driving by. The loggers were losing their livelihoods. The TV viewers imagined the owls' deep-set eyes watching as each tree fell. Wasn't an owl a symbol of wisdom? The voices asked: is a person more important than a symbol of wisdom? Is a tree more important than the things you can make from a tree—a table, a house, a fire? The plot thickened. People began living in trees. The voices asked, who really belongs on the endangered species list—spotted owls or loggers? A person living in a tree asked, was the last great auk greatly lonely? But as time passed, the voices subsided, the people came down out of the trees, and the furor over the spotted owl died down and was almost forgotten. And by then everyone knew: both owls and loggers belonged on the endangered species list. * And then, one day, a voice sounded again. It announced that the habitat of tigers was shrinking to extinction. Then more voices: The habitat of elephants was shrinking to extinction, the habitat of polar bears, of monarch butterflies, of rhinoceroses, of whales, of wolves, of giraffes, were all shrinking to extinction. National parks were endangered, forests were being deforested, the arctic ice cap was de-icing, the oceans were saturated with plastic, the earth itself should be placed on the endangered species list. The voices were now e-mails which were transmitted on computers and phones that were junked every few years and that stored billions of selfies, some with endangered animals, many of food from small farms that are endangered, stored on server farms, which are flourishing. It takes a nuclear reactor ten days to generate the energy to store photos of people's food on the Cloud for one day. The Cloud was flourishing, clouds were polluted. Selfies with pandas were flourishing, pandas were endangered. Amazon was flourishing, half the trees in the Amazon rainforest faced extinction. Facebook flourished harvesting faces. * The e-mail voices asked, Could we please chip in? Could we please send ten dollars to Save the Trees, Save the Alaskan Wilderness, Save the Indonesian Rainforests, Save the Grand Canyon, Save the Great Barrier Reef, Save the Galapagos Islands, Save Vermont's Rivers, Save the Gulf of Mexico, Save the Kenyan Savanna, Save the Arctic, Save the Antarctic? Could we please do something, anything, besides stroking the feathers of the memory of the quaint furor over the spotted owl while lounging on the ruins of nostalgia?

People were getting rid of their libraries, and they sighed with relief when they spoke of it, as though the weight of all those books had long been more burdensome than they could bear. Companies had long since downsized their workforces; governments had streamlined offices and services; now a general reorganizing frenzy took hold of the populace, who wanted to be freed of the clutches of matter—books, records, files, CDs, shoeboxes full of photographs and negatives, cartons stuffed with cards and letters in envelopes in a confusion of sizes with handwriting legible and illegible, blue, black, violet, etiolated blue. How orderly were e-mails! Lined up in neat rows, all in the same sans serif typeface, immaterial, contained in an inbox that wasn't really an inbox, just the digital simulacrum of one. Everyone had had enough of texture. There had been millennia of texture, of aristocrats' writing boxes, now in museums, crammed with ink bottles and quill sharpeners and beribboned letter paper, lined in dark blue velvet and chased in silver, with secret compartments jammed with yet more matter, love letters and IOUs and vials of laudanum, that were kept on rolltop desks honeycombed with dozens of drawers and pigeonholes filled with seals—scissors—pins—letter openers—paper clips—tins of wax—invoices—drafts—and assorted other ephemera. Oh, who needed it? Who needed more than a plank on sawhorses on which sat a laptop loaded with a digital copy of *Being and Time*? Let the museums have the rest of it, repositories of our collective marcescence. Unburdened by objects, people would at last slip through life like marbles down a polished staircase. Unburdened by shops, the streets would break free of narrative, the glass towers loft auspiciously weightless. * Only a few deluded sensualists still mad for matter were full of misgivings. They wandered, bewildered, with ink-stained hands among their overflowing bookshelves dusky as dioramas of the ruins of nostalgia.

When we were in Berlin, we stopped and got coffee at Starbucks. When we were in London, we stopped to get coffee at Starbucks. When we were in Beijing, we stopped and got coffee at Starbucks. When we were in New Delhi, we stopped to get coffee at Starbucks. When we were in Seattle, we stopped to get coffee at the original Starbucks in Pike Place Market, but the line wound around the block. So we walked one block east to the next Starbucks, a non-original Starbucks, where there was no line at all, and we stopped and got coffee, then resumed our walk, talking about authenticity, origins, belonging, reproducibility, Melville, the local, the glocal, frappuccinos, the English language, the Italian language, what kind of world it is where "tall" can mean "small," portmanteaus, the white whale, the chaste mermaid, feathers in foam, access, distributed sameness, the history of sugar, and home. * We got so caffeinated we did not notice the six more Starbucks we passed on our walk—nor, like ghostly overlays, the ruin after ruin of what had been there before, quietly foaming in immanent nostalgia.

We were clicking through photos of a lost Mongolian tribe on the internet on our laptop after work. We had clicked on the click-bait headline "lost Mongolian tribe" and were looking at a photo of a girl clutching a baby reindeer like a stuffed animal, bathing it in a lake. We were considering the symbiotic relationship of the lost Mongolian tribe to reindeer, while looking at a photograph of a human baby asleep propped on a furry flank. We were thinking about anthropology, and about the paradox of the observed observer, and wondering how a Mongolian tribe can be lost if it has already been found by the observed observer, who has lost her own glass eye of objectivity when she has found what it is she wanted all along to see. We were imagining anthropologists observing our own behavior, noting down our symbiotic relationship to our laptop, noting down the number of clicks we expend on click-bait hoping to satisfy our nostalgia for symbiotic relationships with animals we've never had, noting down our nostalgia for the possibility of living lost, not found. Cities had for a century and a half permitted some of us to live lost, but forces beyond our control were now insisting that we live found.   *   Under the final photograph it was written that the lost Mongolian tribe survives on money from tourists, on observed observers who come to take rides into the past on symbiotic reindeer. So, like videos marked "rare" that are uploaded to the entire internet, the lost Mongolian tribe was never lost at all. And that's the thing: the observer is always the observed, and the observed the observer, in the ruins of nostalgia.

They lived in a city so full of recent arrivals that nostalgia emerged as an ordering organizational principle, a byproduct of which was that some people were nostalgic for other people's pasts. An imaginary diagram ensued, graphic-designed in pale salmon pink, of which pasts were more liable to be borrowed when people retreated into their skulls as into little darkened palaces made of stiffened sugar. The age of simulacra had either drowned like a city sacrificed to a dam or had simply reproduced itself, and no one was the wiser. Someone was nostalgic for someone else's past who was nostalgic for someone else's past who was nostalgic for someone else's past who was nostalgic for the depiction of the past in a novel by a novelist who had recently ceased to exist. Or had he? As the plaster Beethoven bust still existed that had been placed on the piano as a joke but when the pianist played Beethoven too vigorously fell off and broke into pieces. "When someone asked him about the meaning of a sonata, it is said, Beethoven merely played it over" (Michel de Certeau). Even the first arrivals had arrived too late for history. And that is the reason for the hierarchies seeping into all the pink strata diagrammed in the ruins of nostalgia.

She saw a dactyliotheca in the museum, a wooden cabinet holding three "books" containing not pages, but dozens of tiny drawers filled with white plaster cameos and intaglios—profiles of queens and goddesses sunk into ovals (intaglio: negative), or raised out of ovals (cameo: positive). Rows and rows of cameo or intaglio profiles, raised or sunk, positive or negative, and she thought of the cheap black-and-white cameo pendants she and her sister had been given in Italy, the pearly profile supposedly "mother of pearl," a new term she hadn't understood—how did pearls have mothers?— but looking suspiciously like plastic, and thought of the cameo role the cameo had played in her life, like her sister's friend Cameo, the three of them little girls in the sunken porcelain bathtub, Cameo with brown braids almost black, the cameo role Cameo had played, playing herself, in profile, in the bathtub, and thought she could make her own dactyliotheca with dozens of drawers full of rows and rows of cameos and intaglios, people who'd appeared and played themselves and disappeared—some positive, some negative—and like the Italian cameo in a drawer somewhere forgotten or rediscovered from time to time and considered—plastic or mother-of-pearl? Positive or negative? What about people who'd played both positive *and* negative roles as themselves? Which was pretty much all of them? * Truth is the mother of beauty, necessity is the mother of invention, plastic is the mother-of-pearl cameos her mother, then young, now old, had given to her and her sister in Italy, in black and white, like the checkerboard marble floors of the palazzos they saw in postcards but never entered, leading to the positive or negative ruins of her nostalgia.

Each time we came back to the city that used to be home, the housing prices had gone up. Did you see the latest? Our relatives said. The old Anderson house across the street went for $xxx,xxx. Three blocks over, they're trying to get $xxx,xxx for a tear-down. Each time we came back to the city that used to be home, more unprofitable bungalows had been torn down, and more modernist boxes that filled the lots had been rapidly thrown up. Bungalow after bungalow was disappearing in a city of bungalows. Garden after garden was disappearing in a city of gardens. Each time we came back to the city that used to be home, there were more profitable modernist boxes and fewer gardens, there were fewer and fewer of the landmarks that helped us remember that this was the city that used to be home. Each time we came back to that city, we thought about houses, we thought about home. We thought about the fact that realtors now called houses for sale "homes." Home after home was disappearing, but "home" after "home" was being rapidly thrown up. Someday soon, new people would be calling these "homes" "home." Would it matter that none of them knew that, four owners back, the unprofitable bungalow on that lot had been owned by the Andersons, and that one afternoon we had watched in horror as old Mr. Anderson fell from a ladder while attempting to prune his blackberry bush, or that one May Day we had picked a bouquet of daisies and dusty miller for old Mrs. Anderson, and then sat awkwardly in her dark living room wishing we were outside playing kickball with our friends? Everyone thinks they got in on the ground floor of time. Everyone thinks they arrived in the city just before the city turned, like the milk that never turns in the city's lattes, like the cream that isn't really cream in the vegan cucumber ice cream. And maybe we did—maybe we did all arrive in the city just before the city turned. Maybe we did all arrive at the best spot in history, just before everything started to go south. And maybe that is why we know that, for now, the only home we can count on is in the ruins of nostalgia.

We went to visit the natural history museum and discovered it was digitizing. The dioramas we used to lose our gaze in were gone—the trompe l'oeil space painted in realistic detail inviting us to forgo the details of the "real" space our eyes were daily fooled by. We couldn't find the stuffed polar bear in his glass case, the badly taxidermied lynx we remembered dangling laxly from a branch, the specimen boxes of butterflies— great spangled fritillaries, brown meadows—whose wings had been chemically treated to unfurl dutifully for the viewer, the artfully arranged aviary with buttons under each bird you could press to hear a tinny reproduction of its call, birds who had sacrificed their lives so that we might live, i.e., acquire knowledge, i.e., the ability to name and identify the birds, their songs, knowledge we did not bury like the stuffed albino squirrel had once buried nuts, but hoarded and made no use of, or felt for in our mental coat pockets from time to time, like the chestnut we kept feeling for in our real coat pocket all fall, long after its saps had evaporated and its living brown had hardened to a dead brown, a tiny nutcase of destiny containing the blueprint of the future tree whose dynasty of leaves it might have founded had we just left it on the ground, as if it granted us access to some knowledge for which we would forever be in arrears, we who had so little access to knowledge of our own future selves—or even of our current selves—for example— why we kept a chestnut in our coat pocket all fall, or why we turned the murderous pages of *Birds of America* enraptured, or why we cried each time we watched the video of the once-famous polar bear rotating in a daze from brain encephalitis before slipping from his artificial ice floe into his artificial ocean, or even why we hunted for the bear's stuffed hull in the museum and finally found it shunted off to a side room, along with the lynx, the dusty butterflies, the silent birds—oh what to do, what to do, with all this matter, piling up in all the side rooms inside us in the ruins of nostalgia.

On childhood road trips she had been hypnotized by the lyric rising and falling of the wires between steel telephone poles shaped like Victorian headmistresses rigid and lonely in the fields. And dreamed of the galvanized cables lying peacefully on the Pacific floor, galvanizing words to worlds. Cords were going the way they had come, speechlessly retreating into the ether, but melancholics and aesthetes browsed the internet at night looking for the kinds of connections only objects from their spun-sugar pasts could forge. * They searched for rotary phones, the kind with the curly telephone cord that always had one kink in it, curling the wrong way or refusing to curl, like the one she'd spent hours as a teenager re-curling with her fingers while lying on the green-carpeted living room floor, trying to learn how to talk on the phone: how to withstand long pauses, how to wind politely down, how to say what she really wanted to say. * The kink had refused to curl, the thing that had wanted to be said kept vanishing when she tried to say it into the phone, like stars that vanish unless you look at them indirectly. The black rotary phone was made of star matter. So many millions of black rotary phones were buried deep in landfills, their cords spiraling and spiraling into millions of silences. Like any phone, they had held out the carrot of communication, but given only the stick of circumlocution. * So didn't they belong heaped among the ruins of nostalgia?

We were trying to find the world before we were born that the loved one had taken with him, a world in his mind he had shown us pieces of from time to time, so that over the years we had fit together a version of this world in our own minds, which had taken on material, if fragmentary, form. Handwritten lists in all caps on graph paper, stories solicited and retold over pumpkin muffins, a whole house secreting photographs and rosaries and bone magnifying glasses belonging to people we could not identify, who were our relatives. When the loved one took his world with him, it turned out that the world in our minds built out of fragments of his world had been mostly dependent on him, like a whole illuminated villa powered by a single generator in the shed intended only for emergencies. The generator suddenly stopped, and the lights of the villa went fragile. Like when someone in a movie turns off a bedside lamp, and another light turns on—cold and bluish. The scaffolding holding up the details faltered; the photographs of strangers with eyes the color of tarnished skies would remain forever photographs of strangers—as one day the photographs of the loved one would depict a tarnishing stranger to others. *The lake that froze over every winter. Streetcars to downtown that had since been dismantled. A hand-built house carried away by a cyclone. The zoo down the street where as a boy he had brushed the ponies.* The loved one took his world with him, a world sovereign to our world yet touching it at every point, a world we had believed we would always be able to reconstruct in our minds. But from that time on, only fainter and fainter reproductions of it could be pieced back together in the ruins of nostalgia.

Nostalgia was invented not long after the first pendulum clock, which increased accuracy sixtyfold over the verge-and-foliot clock. Which seems not-insignificant. When bells structured time, time was benevolent and invisible. Windows in houses establish an inside and an outside. Mirrors look into mirrors and consider themselves in infinitely beveled regress. Even the digital clock loves its own structural abruptness. When the present looks back at the prearranged past and adores it in a mise-en-abyme of feeling, the prearranged past can luxuriate into the post-arranged moment after the events have gone through their spellbinding mother-of-pearl-handled sieves of happiness, littering time pieces along the cognitive shore. Nostalgia was invented, like time was invented, like windows were invented, like adoration was invented. There is no kinder face than the round, disinterested face of the clock, encircling and circulating its recurring version of history, nevertheless so singular. When bells structured time, time was hollow and hieratic, calling the faithful to their regularized hours of adoration in an eternal present of annular unction. The bells have never stopped ringing in the ruins of nostalgia.

We traveled to a walled city, the kind we had seen in medieval paintings, and felt snug at night inside the bed, which was inside a room, which was inside an apartment, which was inside a building, which was inside the walled city. For the first time in a long time we felt that we were inside, not outside. For the first time in a long time we were pretty sure that we were indisputably inside. At first we did not hear the ticking of the little plastic alarm clock, but soon we were listening to it with ever increasing alarm, because we wanted it to be always nighttime, with the gates to the city shut and us snug inside the walled city, inside the building, inside the apartment, inside the room, inside the bed, inside the walled city of our minds. In the daytime, the gates to the city would be flung open, and the inside would no longer be clearly demarcated from the outside. In the daytime, the gates would be flung open, and we would remember that we did not know who had the heavy golden key to the city. Lying awake in the bed all night it was hard to remember what being outside the walled city had felt like. We tossed the plastic alarm clock out the window, but could still hear it ticking from beyond the wall of the city. We pictured the long verdigris rampart descending to wherever. * We wanted everyone to be able to feel this feeling, of being inside, but the walled city was small, and there were only so many buildings, apartments, rooms, and beds, and only so much room inside the walled city of our minds. And anyway, we were granted our two ecstatic, sleepless nights inside, and then we too found ourselves once again indisputably outside, headed home to our habitual vigilance in the exposed ruins of nostalgia.

"There's nothing more invisible than a memorial," wrote Robert Musil, but really there's nothing more invisible than history, which a memorial attempts (in vain) to make visible. But isn't there one thing more invisible than history: history that has been erased? And isn't there one thing more invisible than erased history: traces of the erasure? And isn't the most invisible thing of all the intention to erase history into invisibility—invisible as glass enveloped by glass swallowed by glass nested inside glass absorbing glass?   *   A burnt orange socialist palace visible only in photographs and mind's eyes was replaced by the reconstruction of an imperial palace that for seventy years was visible only in photographs and mind's eyes, because it had been replaced by the burnt orange socialist palace. And now this history is invisible.   *   Is the mind's eye like the fly's compound eye: compartmented, compartmentalizing, inscrutable, voracious, keeping its multifarious intentions and devotions to itself?   *   Nostalgia, too, is invisible, but the products of nostalgia are not invisible. How many palaces have been reconstructed, palaces dismantled, history books recalibrated, pasts erased, pasts pastelized, gardens re-fluffed into velleity on its fumes? Remembering is one of the few political acts both radical and tedious. Never invisible are the memorials mounted in the ruins of nostalgia.

We felt nostalgic for how we used to get obsessed from time to time by a snatch of song playing over and over in our heads that we could not identify. We might hear the snatch of song float from a stereo through an open screen door, or drift over to us from the window of a passing car, and we'd enter into a state of harmonic tension. The snatch of song would creep into and conquer our heads of its own accord, a song we'd heard once, or many times, a long time ago, or last week. The snatch of song we could not identify was like an itch we could not scratch. The itch was erotic, as all itches are erotic. The notes would play over and over again in our heads like a code offering and refusing to be cracked at the same time (to reveal what?), or like a half-voluntary, half-involuntary soundtrack to our own emotional volition. What internal drive was playing the snatch of song in our heads over and over? Knowing we did not know the name of the song, knowing we had no way to hear the song as a function of our will, knowing we were at the mercy of a sequence of notes either obsessively repeating or that we obsessively repeated, a formulaic key to fit the dark lock opening up all forms? * One snatch of song would be replaced by another snatch of song in due time; and thus we moved through scenes with fits and starts of fragments injecting phatic sense into our lives. * Now all you had to do was type in "sure + hell + retaliate" and the internet would promptly scratch your itch, and an entire structure of desire would deliquesce into the ruins of nostalgia.

If desire is a remittance economy whose currency is earned abroad and spent domestically, then what is nostalgia? A dysfunctional gift economy whose items stop circulating when recollections are collected into infinitesimal trunks that glitter once and then are sunk to the bottom of the mind for safekeeping. Desire exports; nostalgia imports and imports and imports. Desire is a component of nostalgia, but only in certain cases is nostalgia a component of desire, and then desire and nostalgia become the two lanes of an endless cloverleaf highway heading every which way to infinity. * Nostalgia keeps looking forward to the past. But what is desire looking forward to? The past reupholstered for future swooning? Is that why the excruciatingly fragile furniture in castles never invites anyone to linger? The inlaid recamiers, the brittle ottomans, the ormolu fauteuils . . . * We watched as heavy royal blue velvet curtains parted on an antiquated scene, to all evidence headed into the future, as every single thing is headed into the future—even nostalgia. Even the ruins of nostalgia.

We felt nostalgic for the abandoned dream of the paperless office. In the paperless office, it was said, all communication was going to be clean of trace, stored in metal. The latent urge to drift in individual sheets would be disciplined, forests would remain uncut. Work would be orderly, armored, inexorable; the fragility of organic matter would, at last, be overcome, in the dream of the paperless office.   *   We felt nostalgic for the paperless office, yes. But what we had forgotten was that because the term "paperless office" was made up primarily of the words "paper" and "office," what we had actually been imagining all along was an office *made* of paper, a dream of endlessly available surfaces we would fill with the inexhaustible ink of our calligraphic minds. In the office made of paper, we would work in the midst of wall-size tablets of paper whose layers upon layers of blankness were not at all blank, but latent with the inkling that some of our beautiful ideas might be prized out of the clouds of our minds and be transcribed, be realized. We would write exposed, ensconced in the delicate constancy of our disconsolate thoughts, for the eyes of those we invited in to our paper(less) office.   *   Like many dreams that have had to be abandoned, the paperless office floated off somewhere, only to lodge in the collective shelving of ideas whose time might or might not ever come. But because it was an active imagining we had passively participated in, we too felt wistful for the abandoned dream of the paperless office, and its unrealized potential. It made us think of our own unrealized potential . . . of how it might have been possible, at one time, to have been a paperless office made of paper. The offices are always open in the ruins of nostalgia.

She was reluctant to admit she felt nostalgic for symmetry. Symmetry for nostalgic felt she admit to reluctant was she. She was a well-schooled modernist. She knew symmetry was just a mindless mirroring of that most atavistic of images—the face. The face of a loved one, or a snow owl, or a saint (none of which were symmetrical, anyway). But what, she wondered, about that little Carnegie library in which she had once spent untold hours doing her homework, modest temple of philanthropy and self-betterment, with its oval windows equidistant to each side of the entablatured front door? Or the reversed birds eyeing each other on Persian carpets entwined in stylized foliage she'd seen in the carpet shop (long since torn down) downtown? Or the perfectly symmetrical Italian Renaissance villas she had looked up on the internet? Or most buildings, gardens, objects, art objects, signage, and public works, up until the twentieth century? Some of which were still circulating their symmetrical disorder? (The Carnegie library was now an antiques mall.)   *   Symmetry had worn out its welcome, she could see that. Like ornament, like swan kings, like voyaging by sea. Like the black rotary phones in the antiques mall. For symmetry, everyone now knew, had been hiding something: interiors that upheld systems of asymmetry. And philanthropy, too, had been hiding something: an interior of misanthropy in the form of disparities it did nothing to reverse. But oh the aphrodisiac of equal distribution, of OH CET ECHO, RUE LA VALEUR—of a symmetry so perfect it atomizes its interior, till there is no more interior, only tiers and tiers of exteriors, mirroring surfaces upon surfaces. (Even software cannot recognize the perfection of the lost loved one's face.)   *   She asked: was it symmetry's fault that it had afforded an orderly façade for systemic asymmetrical disorder? It *was* probably philanthropy's fault that, in a just world, it would not exist. She asked: now that everyone lived in asymmetrical houses, and worked in asymmetrical buildings with asymmetrical public art in trapezoid plazas, were power structures any more symmetrical than when symmetry had hidden asymmetry? — Or were we, as she suspected, just left with an unjust world trashed with lopsided stuff?   *   She took refuge in the antiques mall, knowing her face was also hiding something: the distorted Picasso face of her true self, distorted with grief and love and desire and inquisitiveness and acquisitiveness and bitterness and confusion and hope . . . as she furtively stroked a black rotary phone in the ruins of nostalgia.

We were nostalgic for the time when the pointillist paintings had looked like autumnal birch trees, rather than for the time when the autumnal birch trees had looked like pointillist paintings. We were nostalgic for the certainty that the bird we heard singing sweetly in the suburban forest was a recording, rather than being certain that what we thought was a recording was actually a bird. We were nostalgic for the care that had gone into the realism of the polyester lilies we had placed our foolish noses in, spoiling for perfume. We were nostalgic for foolishness, because it meant wisdom might matter. We were nostalgic for fakery, because it meant realness might matter. We were nostalgic for trompe l'oeil, for fool's gold, for crocodile tears, for Mercator globes, for mimeographs, for velveteen, for signifiers unmoored from signifieds. We were nostalgic for the hand-painted cracks in the artificial marble in the ruins of nostalgia.

We wished we could remember when exactly we had realized we were watching the slow and seemingly irreversible dismantling of the American middle class. Oh we could still see it, like an afterimage of a thing that had really existed, in the rearview mirror of history, that is, in the rearview mirror of the Toyota minivan driving its middle-class family into the sunset. We could still see its vast proportions, its infinitely accommodating edges—the way it had always had ample room for everyone—the children of mechanics, the children of schoolteachers, the children of lawyers. There we all were, in our Toyota minivans, driving into the sunset, into "bureaucratic egalitarianism" (Gayatri Spivak). For a brief blip in history, in this certain time and place, people were not either rich or poor, but rich or middle-class. And even if people were rich, they were often, still, middle-class. And those who weren't doing too well—well, they were just cresting up into the middle class, they were "lower" middle class. Never before in history had the middling middle looked so progressive—*Vorwärts*, straight to the midpoint. Was it this yawning amorphousness, this inability or unwillingness to make distinctions, that had doomed the American middle class to less than a century of flourishing, or was that what had allowed it to survive for so long? Ours is a world that has proven itself to prefer more stringent divisions.   *   You could say we had lost ourselves in the middle class, but you could also say we had found ourselves in the middle class.   *   We missed it, even though it was not yet entirely gone. We missed it so ferociously we would drive our Toyota minivans in circles looking for it—forever, if necessary—around the ruins of nostalgia.

We called them "tennis shoes" even though they weren't worn to play tennis, in fact we'd never learned to play tennis, might not so much as ever have held a tennis racket in our hands, but still we wore tennis shoes throughout our childhood, to run through the neighborhood nights for hide-and-seek, to play softball or tetherball, to walk around the lake, and it wasn't until we left to sync ourselves up with the wider world that we understood it would be necessary to drill "tennis shoes" out of our vocabulary and train ourselves to say "sneakers" instead. It wasn't until we had extracted ourselves from our native soil that we were able to perceive the illogic of tennis shoes that were not actually meant for tennis, that were meant for any sport, or no sport at all, but sometimes we still thought *tennis shoes* when we saw that type of shoe in a shop window, or in our own closets, we had never warmed to the word *sneakers*, but you had better believe we used it without fail, we knew our provinciality was leaking out all over us from a thousand holes we couldn't even see, and as we didn't want to be provincial, as we wanted to stand at the center of the universe with our feet clad in sneakers, as we did not want to be peripheral or irrelevant, in tennis shoes, as we did not want to be local, locatable, as we wanted to move smoothly through the sleek corridors of total mobility, with no part of us catching, no element sticking, we did not wish to reveal what we did not wish to reveal. * But now that we had spent so many years sanding down our own specificity, we were starting to question our contribution to the demise of this bit of illogical terminology still used to the end by those who had once tied our tennis shoes onto our feet, then taught us to tie our own tennis shoes, then wore blank looks on their faces when we returned home from the wider world and said "sneakers"—then left, taking "tennis shoes" with them. Our provincial city was no longer provincial, all the people who said tennis shoes were disappearing, and soon no one would remember the little specific illogic of people saying *tennis shoes* for shoes that were not meant for tennis. But we remembered. And we kept "tennis shoes" in a little territory inside of ourselves that was only for ourselves, a territory we would never cede or relinquish or trade away to the wider world, a selvage on the border of our self, one tiny bulwark against the overwhelming sea we ourselves had invited to annihilate us, one islet of intactness in the ruins of nostalgia.

Nostalgia began as an illness with a prescribed cure: opium, leeches, a view of the sufferer's home Alps. But over the centuries it turned into a feeling with no cure— except, perhaps, the feeling itself. What is a feeling? Isn't it a kind of miniature illness, a force that takes hold and keeps us moored inside ourselves, with consequences and a duration we can't foresee? Now that nostalgia was no longer an illness, but a feeling, was it a good or bad feeling? And did we feel we felt nostalgic, or was it a mezzanine of the mind we meandered down to willfully, more an act of will than an emotion? We weren't sure if a feeling could be an act of will, or if it was always a mental reactivity, a reaction to a stimulus—the view of a city we abandoned, to which we cannot return; a photograph of a missed loved one—that only comes under our control when we shift our thoughts, like a roomful of heavy cardboard boxes that must be moved to another room. A roomful of heavy cardboard boxes of regret. A roomful of heavy cardboard boxes of grief. Nostalgia, on the other hand, felt weightless, a tiny black-lacquered snuffbox inlaid with golden scenes, beautiful and detrimental, that we could carry with us effortlessly from room to room, and even out into the world waiting to infect us with feeling. Like Proust's division of memory, can we speak of both voluntary and involuntary feeling? Can we speak of good-bad feeling?   *   Mostly our nostalgia felt involuntary, but sometimes we weren't sure. "People feel with their hearts," wrote Emily Brontë. But maybe sometimes people feel with their minds, especially when, their minds infected with regret or grief, they wander for healing into the feelingly ruined ruins of nostalgia.

We were nostalgic for ruins, but did not want to be ruined by our nostalgia. As revolutions, as abstraction, as automation kept ushering us into the future, we kept wandering back to the past, thinking of cities built up module by module into complexities of verticality leavened by staircases welling up through story after story made possible by the Otis elevator, the staircase's metaphysical bête noire. Increasingly, among the construction sites, we found ourselves thinking *Stay, thou art so fair.* The rich once took the grand tour to Rome to sketch the ruins of the Colosseum; aristocrats built "ruined" follies on the grounds of their peacock-laced estates. We led our visitors to the ever fewer ruins in our city crumbling unobtrusively in the midst of ruthlessly renovated façades. It's what the visitors wanted to see—it made them feel a curve in the doctrine of linear progress that curved their own doctrines of linear progress into something so curvaceous their minds turned for a time into spiral staircases winding indolently past the Otis elevators falling and falling. We led our visitors to the ruins and we overheard them murmuring *Stay, thou art so fair.* We were not rich, but in our heart of hearts we were aristocrats. And for a time decay had held its own amid the otherwise precise façades of commodity fetishism. For that's what decay lacked—precision, or, it was precision that lacked decay. * But we lived in commodities, like cowrie shells. We lived in symbols. And then one day we were expelled. For it turns out one *can* live in a symbol, but only for so long. It turns out only real aristocrats can afford to love ruin. It turns out only those who believe in their own future covet antiques. It turns out only ruined nostalgists can afford the ruins of nostalgia.

It got harder and harder over the years to keep the ruin kept as a reminder of the horrors of war in its designated state of ruin. With time, the ruin did what ruins do: kept further ruining. It is in this way that symbols resist what they symbolize. A jagged verdigris steeple bitten off by a bomb ruining down to the threshold beyond which the symbol turns into the opposite of a symbol—the thing itself. The bomb was the thing itself, presumably—the war was the thing itself (even though it was fought in theaters), but the bitten-off steeple was no longer the thing itself, and the church it somberly crowned was a symbolic church, to which flocked not the faithful, but the ambivalent. But—is the opposite of a symbol the thing itself? Or does the thing itself inhabit the interior of the symbol like a ruin, a ruin kept ruined unto perpetuity, like a piece of amber in which is embedded not the expected fly but the ruin of a fly, unexpectedly not immortal. As the decades passed, the jagged verdigris steeple bitten off by a bomb was regularly repaired but not rebuilt, reinforced but not reimagined, held but not healed. The healing is regularly postponed in the ruins of nostalgia.

In Renaissance paintings, time could be articulated architecturally, so that scenes from the life of the Virgin Mary were divided into rooms she left behind like eggshells her life kept cracking out of. Do we all crack out of our lives as we live on, trying to understand what we have lived through in retrospect as spatial? The architectonics would correspond to events as little as a schematized subway map corresponds to the tracks we make crisscrossing the city looking for love, money, affirmation, transformation. You can't stuff the contents of an eggshell back into a broken eggshell. The scenes of the Virgin Mary's life did not progress on a chronological plane but occurred simultaneously, all at once. But the pasts we have cracked out of can't be idealized if we can't turn around and look at them getting smaller and smaller in the distance behind us. Was the little Maria suckling baby Jesus in one vaulted room nostalgic for the little Maria two vaulted rooms over quietly reading her book of hours while the annunciating dove hovered into the scene with its irreversible message? The gold rays streaking into her heart foretold the coming linearity of the ruins of nostalgia.

As we sat at home clicking on click-bait, we felt nostalgic for newspapers. Down the street a journalist we knew sat at home clicking on click-bait, as she waited for a website to offer her more than "great exposure." The populace clicked and clicked on click-bait. We heard the quiet clicking, but we no longer heard the thwack of the newspaper hitting the screen door in the still-dark morning, which had awakened the dog, which had barked, which had woken us up. We had paid for the newspaper to be delivered. And we were awake, and Mr. Coffee had made us a pot of coffee, and in the dark we were ready for the newspaper and its perfectly solved puzzles of columns. We were ready for deep background. We were ready for protected sources. We were ready for the inverted pyramid, for "allegedly," for "reportedly." We were ready for "objectivity." We were ready for the fourth estate. We were ready for values that tried to adhere to the Geneva Conventions, the Human Rights Charter, the ideals of the Enlightenment— even if they often failed. We had had to wait since the previous morning, and we were ready. We were reading exactly what our neighbors were reading. We were engaging in civic acts. We were in love with the utopia of distribution. We did not believe everything we read; we believed ourselves well-informed.   *   And then came the dismantling of the news desks, the consolidation and then implosion of regional newspapers, the auctioning off of our hometown newspaper's offices, the stilling of the rotating globe on the roof, and then its sale.   *   We did not miss inky fingers, but we did miss the rustle of the overly large pages.   *   We were nostalgic for newspapers we would no longer pay for, as we clicked and clicked on free click-bait in the ruins of nostalgia.

Two turn-of-the-century train stations once provided ornamental ingress and egress to a single large city. One was torn down, and one was restored. But at both sites, something is missing. The commuters entering the dim misshapen warren that replaced the torn-down turn-of-the-century train station might notice the missing grandeur of departure, while the people exiting the restored turn-of-the-century train station might notice the vanished program of optimism for the arriving future—in which antiquated train stations are not restored, in which the past is not refurbished and retrofitted and reified, because it is universally and deliriously understood that the future is going to be so good that it's going to demolish the past (if only by virtue of the fact that it has not yet had the chance to get fucked-up.)   *   As for us. All too often, we felt like the future was a train that was always just leaving the station with us not on it. And so we understood the endless tussle between hopes for the future and hopes for the past, we felt in our own infrastructure why every city we knew was a permanent construction site, here demolishing and there restoring, here restoring and there demolishing. For we, too, were a permanent construction site, permanently trying to understand when an edifice should be torn down, or restored—or, when to break ground to start erecting something new. *   We didn't want to perambulate and perambulate under a vaulted verdigris ceiling hermeneutic with stars considering the constellations as consolation for a world we ourselves were unable, despite all our efforts, to diagram. Oh we had tried and tried to enter the geodesic domes and the modular pods, but we kept falling backward into the ruins of nostalgia.

Scenes from the lake near our childhood home had built up in our minds over the years not like geological strata neatly stacked in chronological order and amenable to labels and arrows, but like a heap of scree that occasionally shifted and then resettled in a different order. Such is the disorderly mind. Funny, isn't it, that we divide the day into hours, minutes, and seconds, time into years, decades, and centuries, the universe into galaxies, history into eras, rock into strata, matter into kingdoms, flowers into cultivars, buildings into rooms full of shelves and flat files and bureaus lined with false-bottomed drawers stuffed with catalogues organized by index card and albums by theme, encyclopedias arranged alphabetically—when the zyzzogeton is at least as important to us as the aardwolf. But the scenes from the lake are disorderly. Like the afternoon we watched a bunch of older kids with unruly hair blasting AC/DC from a tape deck, wearing tube tops and cutoffs, sitting on striped towels smoking cigarettes and sipping Slurpees they'd probably spiked from a stash in the car. How to file away this scene, which pops into our minds from time to time, the blasting of the AC/DC with its terrible and irresistible carnal knowledge into our prepubescent body, along with a faint bell of the desire to both turn into and *not* turn into one of those shaggy older kids, doing god knows what and going "nowhere," already inducted into the halls of "screwing" and pot-smoking and driving their big, stupid cars too close to the edge of the bluff? Oh the bluff, the bluff—the bluff was nowhere near the lake, what a shitty collagist memory is, the bluff with its cargo trains rumbling along its base, its buff crest towering behind the gray-sand beach, it was a couple of miles away from the lake—and suddenly we think, maybe the AC/DC kids weren't *at* the lake—but no, we tell ourselves, the AC/DC kids *were* at the lake, the AC/DC kids will be at the lake till the end of time, at least until the end of our time (what other time is there?), the AC/DC kids *were* at the lake, with their indestructible bodies and their deflowered nervous systems flooded with the drug of their enviable insolence, the boys with their turbulent hair, the girls in terrycloth tube tops will be at the lake, in their yellow or orange or hot-pink tube tops, the yellow or orange or hot-pink Slurpees, the blue Slurpees, and the mind with so little organizational redress in the ataxic mess of the ruins of nostalgia.

We sensed that we were mistaking our world-weariness for wisdom, but we didn't know how to sift one from the other, we didn't know how to extract disillusionment from the ability to see the world with no illusions. The world, it seemed, was still honeycombed with traps, but we no longer fell into most of them. But if we didn't give in to "persuasion architecture"—the candy hearts arranged right next to the cash register—did that mean we had also sacrificed a certain ability to surprise ourselves with our own weakness? Surely a susceptibility to strategically placed sweetness sweetened our own stringencies. Oh the reward centers in the brain, imploding with impulse sugar. * If we were merely world-weary and not wise, how come we knew that revolutions eat their young, that lotuses are actually just onions, that *erst kommt das Fressen, dann kommt die Moral* (Brecht)? We knew the turquoise globe was dependent on a stand, a housing, or a cord, and we also knew it could slip away from us if we failed to hold onto it with the appropriate awe. * Was our nostalgia a symptom of our world-weariness, or was it a sign that we were finally wise enough to build our own factory-palaces of synthetic happiness churning out candy hearts in our minds? We were wise to the synthetic, but in our world-weariness—or our wisdom?—we allowed it in. We were wise to nostalgia, but in our world-weariness—or our wisdom?—we allowed it in. Butter might not have melted in our mouths, but that didn't mean all our orifices were not of ice. We were wise to flattery, to certainty, to historicity, but we lay down our burdens for all of them. We were wise to ourselves, in every sense. We were wise to hearts, candy or otherwise. We were world-weary, but we were wise enough to our world-weariness to succumb to the attractions, and the repulsions, of the ruins of nostalgia.

An eight-story building filled with textile workers in Bangladesh collapsed because its top four stories were built illegally. The news showed dead girl after dead girl laid out in rows, but did not show the living people in Europe still streaming into the stores selling the clothes made by the garment workers, now dead. There was no blood on the T-shirts, no blood on the bikinis, no blood on the pants or dresses or jackets heaped in four stories in bags nearly bigger, sometimes, than living girls. The news-consuming world gasped, and then a corporation or two breathed out a furtive sigh for the days before the internet, when buildings far away with four illegal stories could simply collapse in silence without other people, far away, having to care, or protest, or think too hard about their shopping habits. For by now it was impossible not to know that real costs might always be shifting, but they never vanish—somebody, somewhere, is always paying the difference of anything sold below its true value. But how is true value determined except by what we are willing to pay? The T-shirt with no blood on it would eventually be shoved into the back corner of a drawer until one day it would be rediscovered and held to the light, unleashing a small flood of nostalgia. * The problem with the eight-story structure that collapsed was structural. The problem with not having to think too hard about one's shopping habits is structural. * The girls from the Bangladesh factories were briefly mourned by the rest of the world, and then forgotten by it. * The eight flattened stories smoked and smoked for a time on the internet, then got consigned like everything else to the ruins of nostalgia.

We felt like nostalgic futurists, one half of our bodies aimed with hope at the prospect of future utopias, one half aimed with dread at the prospect of future utopias, torquing ever backward at an inexorably receding past. Take the green roof, the greenfield, the greensward, the greenwashing effects of green how I love you green. We wanted to be saturated in this new world of green, but wasn't it just the old world of green, for which everyone had long been nostalgic, in new guise? We sat on our balconies overlooking the green roofs of the city, noting that the rate of rediscoveries that seemed like discoveries seemed to be increasing. Maybe looking forward was actually, depending on your standpoint in history, looking backward, or the reverse. What *was* certain, from the perspective of our balconies, was that everything was always receding. If we could look, instead, into a sphere, like an idealized medieval peasant, would we see all that it was requisite to see: the four seasons succeeding each other with reassuring regularity all around us—interrupted only by the occasional seven years' war or harvest moon—till we too were rotating in a rotund cocoon of regularized reiterations? A cocoon, or a vacuum? Were our cocoons actually vacuums, our vacuums cocoons, were we emerging from emptinesses only to empty into emptinesses, the way even green is a temporary ink injected into the leaves of the city's green roofs it then recedes from, leaving us with the incessant recessions of the ruins of nostalgia?

We felt nostalgic for libraries, even though we were sitting in a library. We looked around the library lined with books and thought of other libraries we had sat in lined with books and then of all the libraries we would never sit in lined with books, some of which contained scenes set in libraries. * We felt nostalgic for post offices, even though we were standing in a post office. We studied the rows of stamps under glass and thought about how their tiny castles, poets, cars, and flowers would soon be sent off to all cardinal points. We rarely got paper letters anymore, so our visits to the post office were formal, pro forma. * We felt nostalgic for city parks, even though we were walking through a city park, in a city full of city parks in a country full of cities full of city parks, with their green benches, bedraggled bushes, and shabby pansies, cut into the city. (Were the city parks bits of nature showing through cutouts in the concrete, or was the concrete showing through cutouts in nature?) * We sat in a café drinking too much coffee and checking our feeds, wondering why we were more anxious about the future than anxiously awaiting it. Was the future showing through cutouts in the present, or were bits of the present showing through cutouts in a future we already found ourselves in, arrived in our café chairs like fizzled jetpacks? The café was in a former apothecary lined with dark wood shelves and glowing white porcelain jars labeled in gilded Latin, which for many years had sat empty. Had a person with an illness coming to fetch her weekly dose of meds from one of the jars once said to the city surrounding the shop, which was slowly transforming into this city, *Stay, thou art so fair*? Weren't these the words that sealed the bargainer's doom? Sitting in our presumptive futures with our hearts pounding, must we let everything run through our hands—which were engineered to grab—into the past? In the library, in the post office, in the city park, in the café, in the apothecary . . . O give us the medicine, even if it is a pharmakon—which, as the pharmacist knows, either poisons or heals—just like nostalgia. Just like the ruins of nostalgia.

We were nostalgic for nostalgia. We missed missing. We longed for the longings of what seemed like long ago. We looked all over for *sehnsucht*. Presence was not always the present it was given to be. * We read Francis Bacon's essay on gardens and gasped for air, drowning in absent presence, in ideated double violets and cornelians and French honeysuckle, the early tulippa, flower-de-luces, the sweet satyrian, and bay hedges 4 foot high—*ver perpetuum*. An everlasting spring. Wasn't nostalgia a version of organized *ver perpetuum*, everlasting spring? Could we not plant the garden plots in our minds such that some image, or the memory of some image, or the missing of the memory of some image was always in flower, so that the frozen bewildering array of the present would always be intervened with by foregone fritillaria and fronds? Or was nostalgia like a pollarded tree whose pruned stumps put forth ineffectual sprigs terrorized by the ruthlessness of design? Isn't nostalgia propelled by a desire for the beautiful so potent that presence is sacrificed for stringent arrangements of absence? Doesn't the nostalgist adore her Claude glass, which requires the viewer to turn her back on reality for the sake of the picturesque? And does she arrange her scenes as prescriptively as Bacon maps out his ideal garden, or is there room for haphazard and ha-has? * Reading Francis Bacon's essay on gardens, we knew we had to write it into a poem, so that later we could reread the poem and feel nostalgic for the first time we had read the essay and been bowled over by Bartholomew-tide. People are always gunning to drag their gardens into the ruins of nostalgia.

We kept replacing a house with a house with a house, thinking we were getting somewhere, elsewhere, but one day we held still for a moment and realized that all of the houses had been accumulating underneath our current house the whole time, one atop the other like a fragile hazardous lighthouse whose weak beacon would never be able to keep us from breaking to pieces on the shoals. Our apartments kept us in pieces: we had segmented ourselves throughout the rooms, our dreams in one room and our nightmares in another, our plans to get somewhere, elsewhere, drifting here and there in precarious piles. If there was no progress, there could be no stasis. If there was no future, there could be no remorse. If there was no original, there could be no copy, only a utopia of copies, everywhere and at all instants like our own inevitable selves, filling selvage after selvage with inevitability. Developers tore down unprofitable houses and replaced them with profitable houses, but the unprofitable houses did not disappear: they accumulated like strata of sedimented geologic time in the minds of those who would never be free of them. But weren't we also obsessed with profit and loss? Trying to get somewhere, elsewhere, yet engulfed with grief, stuck in the very same plot we believed we'd set out from? If there was no replacement, there could be no retracing. If there was no development, there could be no ruin. If there was no mobility, there could be no nostalgia. There could be only a mise-en-abyme of home.

"Nostalgia is at the core of the modern condition," wrote Svetlana Boym. But if that is the case, then why are some modern people not nostalgic? Is everyone "modern" just by virtue of being alive? No matter how old-fashioned our old-fashioneds, our superannuated utopias, our antique ideations of egg creams.   *   We confessed we felt nostalgic for egg creams, although we had never drunk an egg cream. Instead, we drank Slurpees, blue Slurpees, from the Woolworth's in the mall we grew up in. First egg creams disappeared, then the Slurpee machines in the Woolworth's disappeared, then the Woolworth's disappeared. And then the mall disappeared. Egg creams, we'd been told, were never as creamy as their name fathoming a creaminess and a frothiness, an impossibly frothy creaminess, the dreaminess of creaminess.   *   Still, it came as a mild shock to learn that there are no eggs, nor is there any cream, in an egg cream. This we were told by a person who is no longer alive, and thus no longer modern. Svetlana Boym is no longer alive. The ruin of the egg cream foams all over the ruins of nostalgia.

Is the ruins of nostalgia a place, or a vanishing point? Nostalgia, writes philosopher Barbara Cassin, is written in the future perfect tense. When the future is perfect, will we know if our heart is a ruin or a vanishing point? Brunelleschi invented perspective in 1413; before that, all vanishing points led straight to the navel of God (in naves of churches). When the future is perfect, we will have understood whether modernity begot perspective or perspective begot modernity, reflected in mirrors set up to echo Euclidean laws of optics for the sovereign eye peering through a bored hole. "The viewer is mirrored in the vanishing point, and thus constructed by it" (Hito Steyerl). When the future is perfect, we will understand why the cities we love are all moving inexorably along the vector of the vanishing point, mirrored but deconstructed. When the future is perfect, Brunelleschi's lost paintings inventing perspective will have been rediscovered, but we will also know that Brunelleschi's invention was only a re-invention of Lorenzetti's painting of perspective in 1342, its ornamental floor tiles receding into the pixelated future it helped construct. When the future is perfect, we will understand why even with perspective and modernity and post-modernity and the internet *and* God, we understand nothing, unto infinity, not even why nostalgia is written in the future perfect tense, which is a contradiction in terms, like a nostalgic futurist, or a constructed or deconstructed self. When the future is perfect, we will have understood why nostalgia is not written in the *past* perfect tense. And when the present is perfect—will we no longer be so ravished to vanish into the ruins of nostalgia?

It was the last unrenovated building in the city, and all who came to inspect its weathering tiers fell (inwardly) to their knees in veneration. When she lay on her bed she could feel everything she'd used to look so ardently forward to fall behind her like old-growth redwoods thundering to the forest floor as the tree-huggers were escorted out of the woods in handcuffs on the back of a logging truck, supine like the lumber. Who in that primordial darkness would have feared the gentle two-by-four? Looking at all the smoothly serene façades to either side of the last unrenovated building, she wanted to understand the ruinousness of renovation, and she wanted to interpellate the romance of ruins, study it, take apart its ethics and its aesthetics and put it back together again with one segment of the egg-and-dart cornice upside down. She wanted the caryatids to crumple over. She wanted people to be decently housed, but she also wanted to cause irreparable damage to narratives of progress washing over the city with their pale blue saline reminiscence of forgetfulness. She wanted to hug the unrenovated buildings until she was led away by handcuffs. She wanted to hug everything she did not want to disappear that would disappear, until she was led away by handcuffs. She lay on her bed, staring, no longer astonished, into the ruins of nostalgia.

We rode in the back of the white Pontiac convertible with its top down, summers, to get to the lake, the mother driving, her two daughters in the back, the mother with her filmy pink scarf over her beehive hairdo tied in a bow under her chin, with her cat's-eye sunglasses, we rode in the back of the white Pontiac convertible with its top down, with the AM radio playing, we rode to the lake, or rather to the wading pool next to the lake, where the mother sent her two daughters into the shallow water and sat on the grass to smoke a cigarette near the other mothers, her eyes behind her cat's-eye sunglasses, we rode on the back of the white Pontiac convertible as it climbed up the stair-like gradations of the hill, and then as it sailed down the stair-like gradations on the other side of the hill, to get to the lake, in the white Pontiac convertible top-down, without seat-belts, perched atop the back seat of the car, up and down the hill, back up, and down, to get to the lake, to get back home, to get to the lake, to get back home, the daughters with their bathing suits coiled tightly in their towels, the father at work, the father driving an hour north to work each day not knowing if he would be driving back to work the next day, the company of the company town laying off three-quarters of its workforce, the mother driving up and down the hills to the lake with the AM radio playing, with her cat's-eye sunglasses, the two daughters perched on the back seat clutching their towels, the brother who knows where, the mother driving, the father driving, the AM radio playing "the bluest skies you've ever seen are in Seattle," the sisters perched on the back of the seat of the white Pontiac convertible with its top down, down and down the stair-steps of the hills and into the ruins of nostalgia.

NOTES

THE RUINS OF NOSTALGIA 8

1. "Wir bleiben alle," which means "We're all staying," is a slogan used by the Berlin squatters' movement that derives from a form of neighborhood organization widespread in former East Berlin, the Wohnbezirksausschuss, or WBA.

2. Umsonst Laden means "free store."

THE RUINS OF NOSTALGIA 9

1.

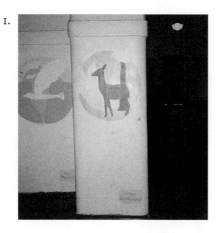

2. The real café was the Last Exit on Brooklyn, in Seattle's University District.

THE RUINS OF NOSTALGIA 15, 49, AND 58

"Stay, thou art so fair" is a translation of Goethe's "Verweile doch, Du bist so schön" from *Faust*. These are the words that, if uttered, would seal Faust's doom and give Mephistopheles his soul:

FAUST:
Whenever to the passing hour
I cry: O stay! thou art so fair!
To chain me down I give thee power
To the black bottom of despair!

"Wir vergessen dich nie" means "We will never forget you," but translates exactly, in German syntax, to "We will forget you never," so that the broken gravestone reads "We will forget you / never."

THE RUINS OF NOSTALGIA 46

"Vorwärts," literally "forward," is the first word in the refrain to the song "Solidaritätslied" ("Solidarity Song"), written by Bertolt Brecht and set to music by Hanns Eisler, which featured in the 1932 film *Kuhle Wampe*.

THE RUINS OF NOSTALGIA 55

"Erst kommt das Fressen, dann kommt die Moral" means "First comes grub, then morals."

ACKNOWLEDGMENTS

Some of these poems were first published, in slightly different versions, in *Conjunctions*, *The Paris Review*, *The Volta*, *Hyperallergic*, *The Spectacle*, *On the Seawall*, *Body*, *Paperbag*, *Oxford Review of Books*, *New American Studies Journal*, and *SplitLevel*. Thank you to the editors.

Some of the poems were published in translation: in German by Andrea Grill in *Literatur und Kritik* and *Stadtsprachen*, and by Joey Bahlsen in *Stadtsprachen*; in French by Stéphane Bouquet in *Vacarme*; in Spanish by Tomás Cohen in *Buenos Aires Poetry* and by Cristián Gómez Olivares in *Op.cit.poesia* and *WD 40: Revista de poesía, ensayo y crítica*; and in Slovak by Ivana Hostová, for Novotvar 2020. Many thanks to these poet-translators.

"The Ruins of Nostalgia 58" appeared in the Poem-a-Day feature on the Academy of American Poets' website, with my thanks to guest editor Brian Blanchfield; "The Ruins of Nostalgia 25" was featured on *Poetry Daily*.

Ten of the poems were published in a handmade chapbook by Catenary Press as *Ten Ruins* (2019). My thanks to Rob Schlegel, Daniel Poppick, and Rawaan Alkhatib.

"The Ruins of Nostalgia 60" was written in response to the sculpture *Untitled, 2011* by Rachel Khedoori, commissioned by Hauser + Wirth's magazine *Ursula*. Thanks to Catherine Davis.

I'm grateful to the Berlin Senate grant program, which in 2018 awarded me a yearlong Work Stipend to focus on this manuscript. Thank you also to the Willapa Bay AiR and the Siena Art Institute for residencies that gave me time and space in which to further it.

My thanks to all the generous friends (and some strangers) who read or listened to versions of these poems and offered comments and/or their thoughts about nostalgia, and in particular to Camille Guthrie, Karla Kelsey, and Sylee Gore. Many thanks as well to John Yau, Bonnie Costello, Nancy Gaffield, Maureen McLane, Mark Levine, and especially to Robyn Creswell for their insights, support, and encouragement. Special thanks to Rae Armantrout. Thanks and love to Rose-Anne Clermont (1971–2022), for whose friendship I will always be nostalgic. And finally, my love and gratitude to John Nijenhuis for accompanying the writing of these poems.

ABOUT THE AUTHOR

Donna Stonecipher is a poet and translator currently living in Berlin, Germany, with an MFA from the Iowa Writers' Workshop. She is the author of six books of poetry, including *The Cosmopolitan*, *Model City*, and *Transaction Histories*, which the *New York Times* named one of the ten best poetry collections of 2018.